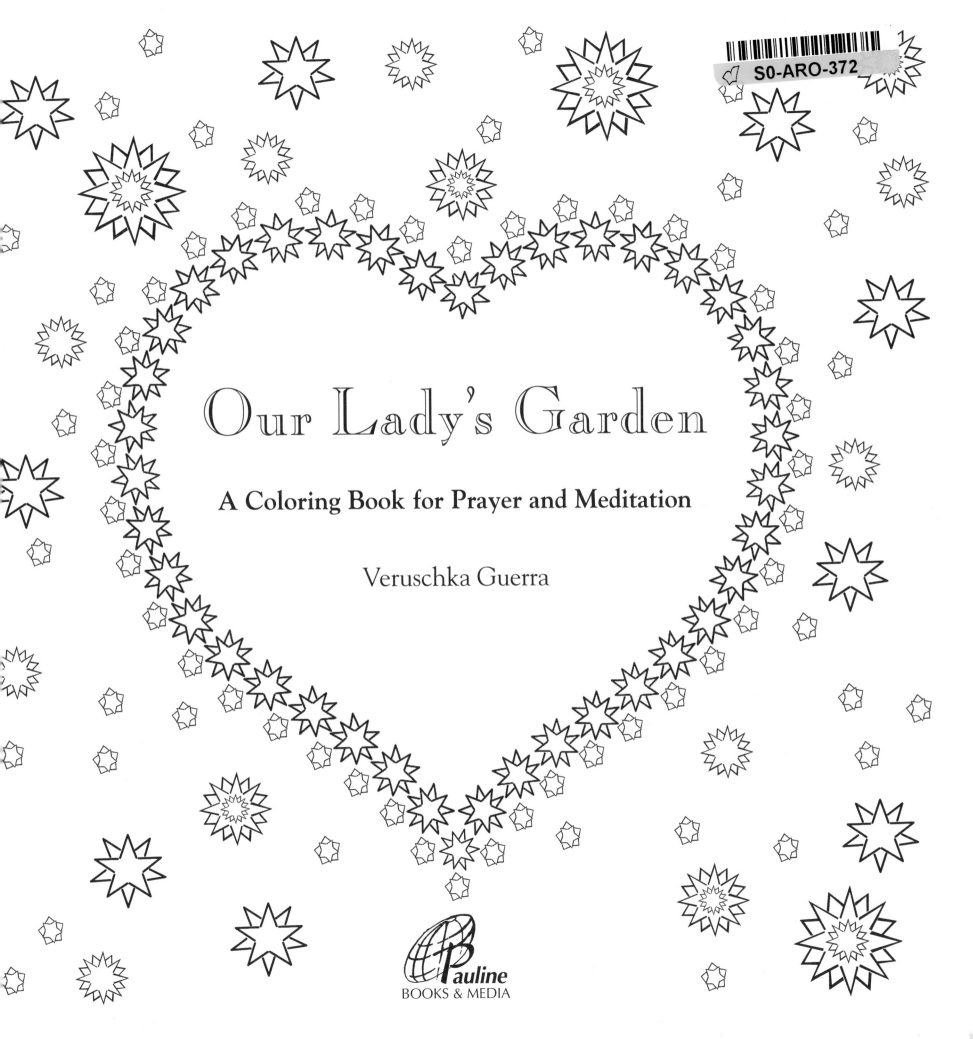

Our Lady's Garden

A Coloring Book for Prayer and Meditation

Veruschka Guerra

Pauline
BOOKS & MEDIA

Book design by Mauricio Pereira

ISBN 0-8198-5501-4

ISBN 978-0-8198-5501-5

Originally published in Portuguese as *O Jardim da Senhora dou Céu* by Editora Santuário 2015—Rua Pe. Claro Monteiro, 342, CEP: 12570-000 – Aparecida-SP

English translation and adaptation by Daughters of St. Paul

Published by Pauline Books & Media, 50 Saint Pauls Avenue, Boston, MA 02130-3491

Printed in Korea

www.pauline.org

Pauline Books & Media is the publishing house of the Daughters of St. Paul, an international congregation of women religious serving the Church with the communications media.

1 2 3 4 5 6 7 8 9   20 19 18 17 16

This book belongs to

_____

Hail Mary

Hail Mary, full of grace
the Lord is with you.
Blessed are you among women
and blessed is the fruit of your womb, Jesus.

Holy Mary, Mother of God,
pray for us sinners
now and at the hour of our death.
Amen.

Hail, Queen of Heaven

Hail, Queen of Heaven.
Hail, Queen of Angels.
Hail, Fruitful Root.
Hail, Gate of Heaven,
from whom the Light of the World was born.
Rejoice, O Glorious Virgin,
most beautiful among all women.
Hail, Radiant Splendor,
and pray for us to Christ.
Amen.

"Jesus wishes to make use of you
to make me known and loved.
He wants to establish in the world a devotion
to my Immaculate Heart. I promise salvation
to those who embrace it; and these souls will be
beloved by God, like flowers placed by me
to adorn his throne."

To the children of Fatima, Portugal, 1917

Consecration to the Immaculate Heart of Mary

O Immaculate Heart of Mary,
full of goodness, show us your love.
May the flame of your heart, O Mary,
descend on all men and women!
We love you beyond measure!
Imprint in our hearts true love,
so that we may desire to seek you incessantly.
O Mary, you who have a gentle and humble heart,
when we fall into sin remember us.
You know that all men and women sin.
Grant that, through your maternal
and Immaculate Heart,
we may be healed of all spiritual ills.
Grant that we may always contemplate
the goodness of your maternal heart
and that we may be converted through
the flame of love in your heart.
Amen.

"Listen and understand well, my little one, nothing should frighten or afflict you.
Do not let your heart be troubled. Do not fear this illness,
nor any other illness, nor anguish. Am I not here? I who am your Mother?
Are you not under my shadow and protection?
Am I not the source of your joy?
Are you not in the folds of my mantle, in the crossing of my arms?
Is there anything else you need?
Do not fear and do not let anything disturb you."

To Saint Juan Diego at Guadalupe, Mexico, 1521

"My Immaculate Heart will be your refuge and is the way that will lead you to God."

To the children of Fatima, Portugal, 1917

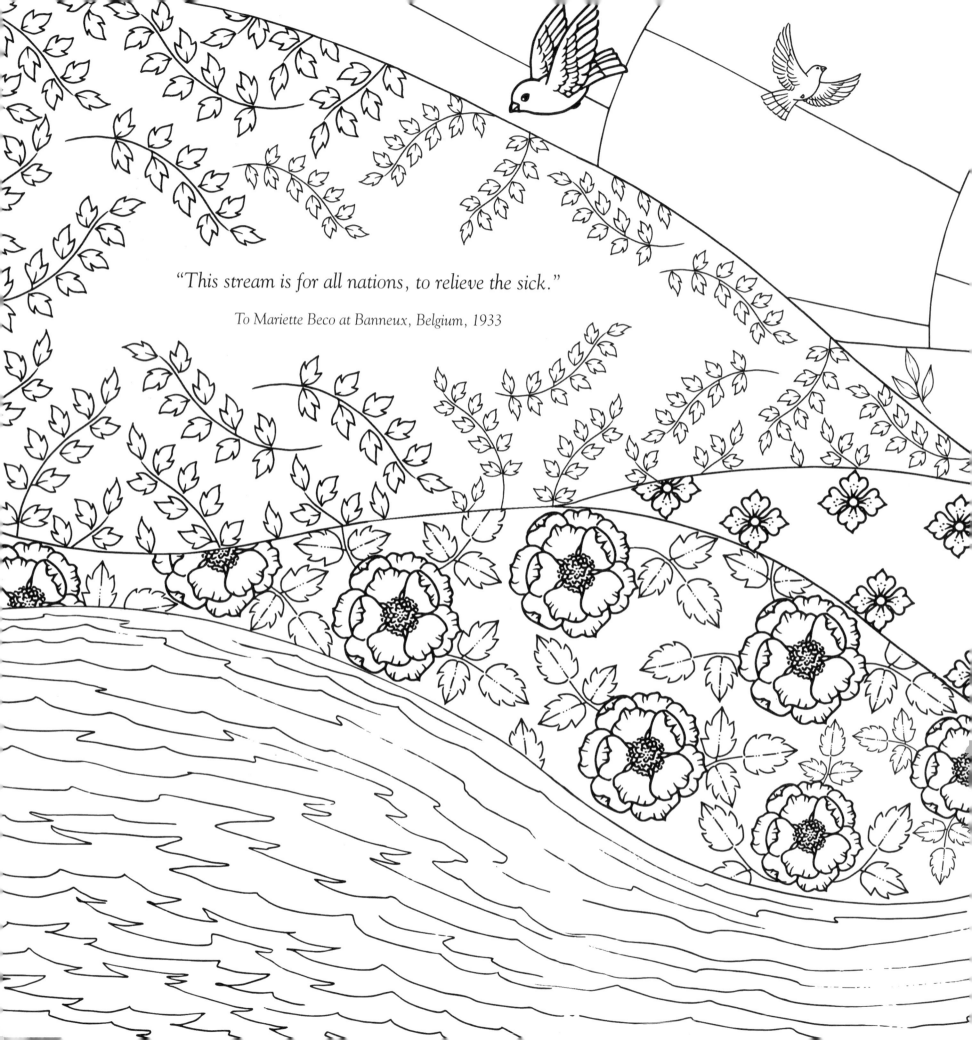

"This stream is for all nations, to relieve the sick."

To Mariette Beco at Banneux, Belgium, 1933

Queen of Peace

Mother of God and our Mother,
Mary, Queen of Peace!
You came here to lead us to God.
Intercede for us so that we too might say:
"Let it be done to me according to your word!"
and follow the Lord as you did.
We place ourselves in your hands
so that amid all the difficulties we face
you may lead us to Jesus.
Through Christ, Our Lord.
Amen.

"But pray, my children.
God will hear you in a little while.
My Son allows himself to be moved."

To several children at Pontmain, France, 1871

"I am the Immaculate Conception."

To Saint Bernadette at Lourdes, France, 1858

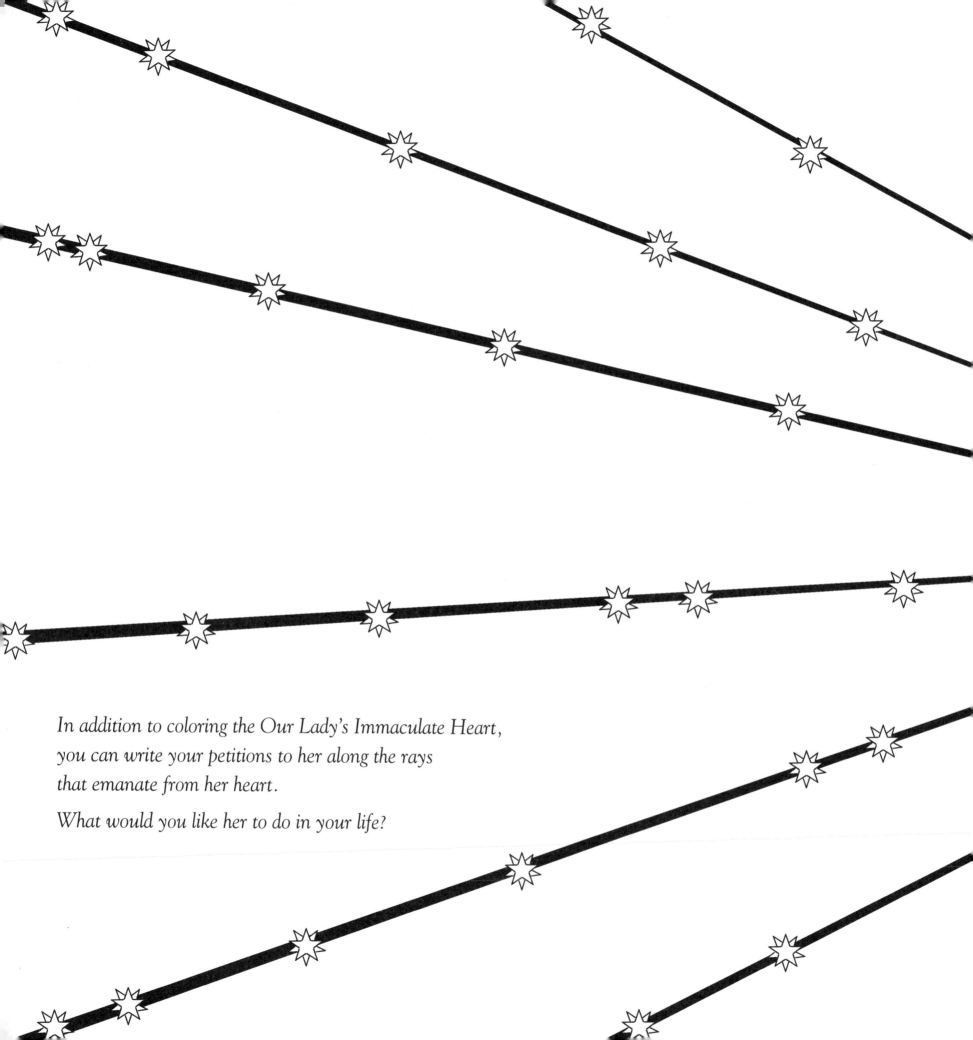

In addition to coloring the Our Lady's Immaculate Heart,
you can write your petitions to her along the rays
that emanate from her heart.

What would you like her to do in your life?

"The rays symbolize the graces I obtain
for all those who ask for them."

To Saint Catherine Labouré at Paris, France, 1830

Mary, Star of the Sea

Hail, O Star of the Sea,
Holy Mother of God,
ever sinless Virgin Mary,
blessed gate of heaven.

That sweet Ave,
from Gabriel's mouth,
gave us grace and peace,
and forever transformed
Eve's name.

Break the sinners' chains,
give light to those in darkness,
Chase all evils from us,
and entreat blessings for us.

Show yourself our Mother.
May the Divine Word,
your Son
who was born for us,
hear our prayers through you.

Oh, most exquisite Virgin,
mildest of the mild,
free us from sin
and preserve us
meek and pure.

Bestow on us a pure life;
make our way safe
until we find in Jesus
joy for evermore.

Praise to God the Father,
honor to Christ in the highest,
and to the Holy Spirit.
Glory to the Trinity. Amen.

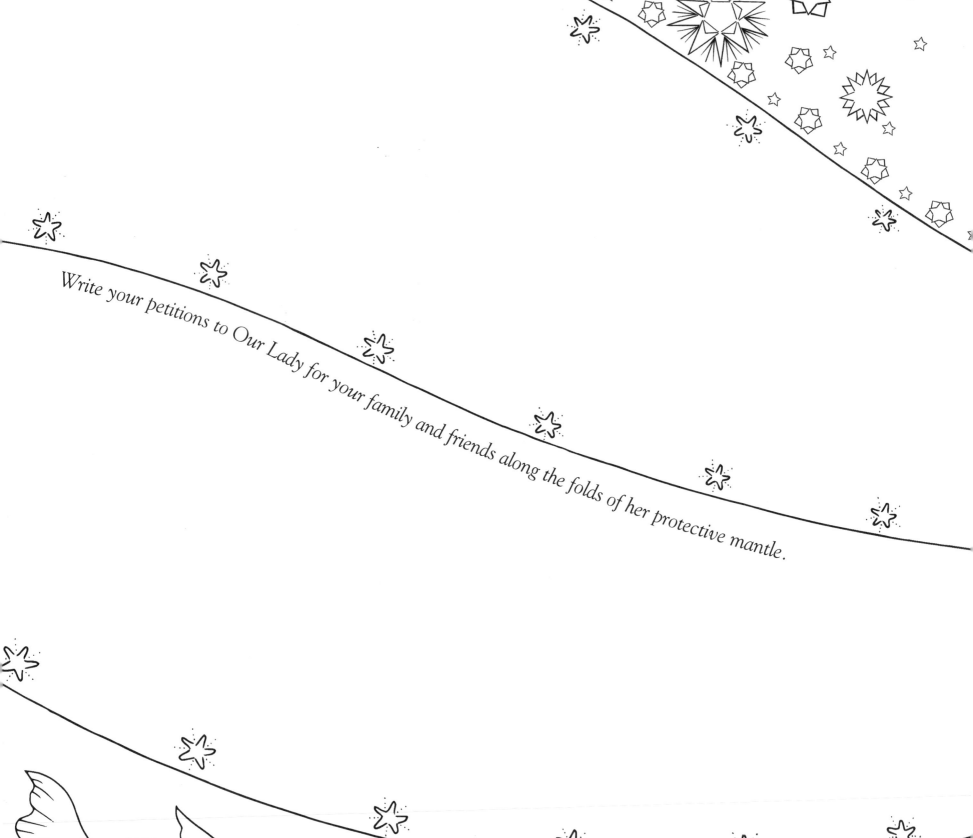

Write your petitions to Our Lady for your family and friends along the folds of her protective mantle.

"I came to relieve suffering.
Have faith in me.
I will believe in you."

To Mariette Beco at Banneux, Belgium, 1933

Regina Caeli

Queen of Heaven rejoice, alleluia.
For Christ, your Son and Son of God,
has risen as he said, alleluia.

Pray to God for us, alleluia.
Rejoice and be glad, O Virgin Mary, alleluia.
For the Lord has truly risen, alleluia.

Let us pray.
God of life, you have given joy to the world
by the resurrection of your Son, our Lord Jesus Christ.
Through the prayers of his Mother, the Virgin Mary,
bring to us the happiness of eternal life.
We ask this through Christ our Lord.
Amen.

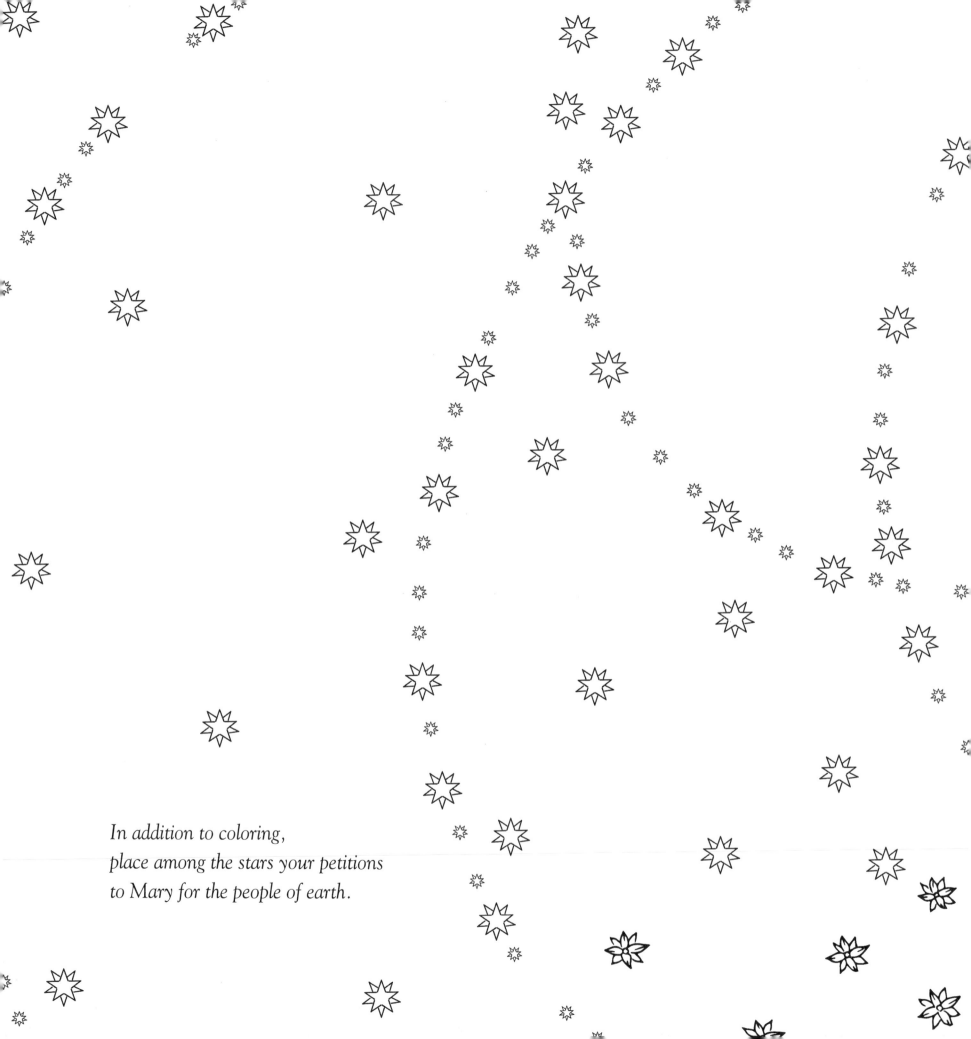

In addition to coloring,
place among the stars your petitions
to Mary for the people of earth.

Invocations to Mary

Soul of Mary, lead me to holiness.
Heart of Mary, inflame me.
Hands of Mary, sustain me.
Immaculate eyes of Mary,
watch over me.
Lips of Mary, speak to me.
Sorrows of Mary, strengthen me.
O sweet Mary, hear me.
In Jesus' heart, hide me.
Never permit me
to be separated from you.
From my enemies, defend me.
In the hour of my death,
call me and take me
to my beloved Jesus,
so that with you I may love and praise him
forever and ever.
Amen.

"Prayer is necessary. Be faithful and fervent in prayer
to console the Master. Pray very much the prayers of the Rosary.
Those who place their confidence in me will be saved."

To Sister Agnes Sasagawa, Akita, Japan, 1973